Original title:
Under the Christmas Tree's Glow

Copyright © 2024 Creative Arts Management OÜ
All rights reserved.

Author: Harris Montgomery
ISBN HARDBACK: 978-9916-94-070-9
ISBN PAPERBACK: 978-9916-94-071-6

Glowing Reflections of Love's Promise

Beneath the twinkling, tinsel strand,
Santa's sleigh might need a hand.
Rudolph's nose is slightly bright,
Did he finish his cookies right?

Memory Lanterns in the Winter's Embrace

The stockings hang with silly glee,
Stuffed with things no one will see.
The cat's climbed high, in the haste,
To knock down ornaments with taste.

The Enchantment of Softly Flickering Lights

Dim twinkling bulbs, a dazzling sight,
The dog thinks it's a midnight fight.
Every sparkle gives a new surprise,
As Auntie dances with pie in her eyes.

Emblems of Joy Tucked Away

Gifts wrapped up with bows that tease,
Eager hands pull back with ease.
Last year's socks still on the flares,
At least I have my Christmas bears!

Melodies of Mirth and Serenity

Tinsel tangled in a cat's tail,
Santa's laugh begins to wail.
Cookies gone, but crumbs remain,
Reindeer games drive the dog insane.

Ornaments hanging on the floor,
Dad's dressed up, but he wants more.
Elf hats placed on grumpy goats,
Laughter erupting like silly quotes.

Gilded Light in Winter's Grasp

Snowballs tossed with little aim,
Uncle Fred's the perfect blame.
Frosty slips and lands in soup,
Everyone bursts out in a loop.

Mistletoe hangs on grandma's hat,
Trying to kiss the family cat.
Pies are flying, oh what a sight,
Dessert's a gamble—risky delight.

A Mosaic of Laughter and Light

Jingle bells and broken toys,
Kids are wild, they're too much noise.
Auntie's fruitcake, oh what a gift,
Taste buds quake, it causes a rift.

Wraps of paper bright and loud,
Cousin tries to bow, oh so proud.
But slip he does on grandma's sock,
Now he's a part of the jolly flock.

Hope's Flicker in the Chilly Air

Lights are twinkling, then they fade,
Dad's confused, the switch mislaid.
Jack Frost scratched on all the panes,
Inside we plotted sticky gains.

Tummy aches from all that cheer,
Someone sneezes, spreads the beer.
Toasting marshmallows caught on flame,
At least we've got a funny name.

Gleaming Gifts of Time and Joy

Bright boxes stacked high, oh what a sight,
Wrapped in strange paper, all shiny and tight.
A cat in the chaos, a dog on the flop,
A holiday mix-up, what a funny swap!

With socks for my brother, and ties for the dad,
A potato for grandma, who'll say it's a fad.
The wrapping is flying like snowflakes in glee,
As we laugh at the jumbles, just wait and see!

Silhouettes of Togetherness and Cheer

The lights are twinkling, the snacks are a mess,
A cookie brigade leads the dogs to confess.
An ornament tumbles, we all let out groans,
Yet laughter erupts, echoing through the bones.

We wear holiday sweaters, in colors so bright,
Competing for laughter, a wonderful sight.
The grandma is dancing, her moves are bizarre,
We join in her rhythm, a merry band star!

The Whispers of Joy Beneath the Boughs

A strange noise erupts, what could it be now?
A raccoon in a hat, eating fruit from the chow.
The laughter erupts as we all take a peek,
It's feasting on cookies, the critter's a sneak!

A surprise from the neighbor, a gift for us all,
A cacti in glitter, just what we can haul.
We laugh 'til we cry at the holiday cheer,
The silly surprises bring us all so near!

Lanterns of Love Amidst Frost's Embrace

The cocoa is splattered, yet everyone smiles,
As strange secret gifts seem to stretch for miles.
An igloo made from snowballs, the kids are quite bold,
While parents just chuckle at stories retold.

With mittens mismatched, and lights in a knot,
We cherish the moments, forget all we bought.
In laughter we gather, as the snowflakes swirl,
Creating new memories, around us they twirl!

Ornaments of Memory and Love

Little baubles dance with glee,
Each one tells a tale, you see.
The cat climbs high, swats an angel,
Down she falls, oh what a tangle!

Laughter rings with every cheer,
As Grandma snags a rogue reindeer.
The lights flicker, we all shout,
"Better not let the dog run out!"

Beneath the Boughs of Joy

Gift wraps crinkle, a mystery prize,
Grandpa's snoring breaks the skies.
The pies are baking, the taste divine,
But where's the wine? Oh, it's mine!

Uncle Joe's jokes go way too far,
While Auntie shows off her new guitar.
The lights twinkle, the cookies sink,
Who needs milk? We've got eggnog to drink!

Radiance in the Silent Night

Twinkling lights compete with stars,
Rabbits play in glittering cars.
Each present wrapped with love and cheer,
But oh, that smell! Is it Pete's old beer?

The snowman's grin turns into a frown,
As Windy McBlizzard comes to town.
With cheeks that glow and spirits bright,
We'll share a laugh, then a snowball fight!

Treasures Hidden in the Green

Beneath the branches, secrets dwell,
Like that last cookie we can't tell!
Ribbons tangled, a sight so grand,
With grandkids giggling, hand in hand.

The fruitcake's sitting all alone,
The dog thinks it's a chewing bone.
The bell rings out, the joy we find,
Together we're a little unrefined!

Shadows of Wrapped Secrets

Jingle bells in crazy flight,
Cats are plotting, what a sight.
Presents stacked, oh what a tease,
Do they smell like tuna, please?

Wrapping paper everywhere,
Mom's lost in a Christmas scare.
Dad has tried to fix a toy,
Now it's just a pile of joy.

Bows go flying, up they soar,
Uncle Joe is on the floor.
Laughter echoes, tinsel flies,
What a sight is this surprise!

Snowmen made from mom's good sheets,
Neighbors laughing from their seats.
Each odd gift wrapped up with cheer,
Guessing games bring holiday beer!

The Hearth's Embrace at Midnight

Footsteps sneak on chilly floors,
Cocoa spills behind closed doors.
Quiet giggles, a sneaky sway,
What a game, we play this way!

Stockings hung, but wait—what's that?
Santa's hat on the old cat!
Whiskers twitch in half a dream,
Presents stuffed, it's quite the scheme.

Just one sip and cookies gone,
Santa's treats all played their role.
Gone are cookies, milk set out,
Now can we just get some clout?

Bright lights twinkle, shadows dance,
Silly hats give us a chance.
In this cozy hearth's embrace,
We trade our toys for silly grace!

Frosted Wishes in the Firelight

Gingerbread men with sprinkles bright,
Hiding snacks, what a delight!
Doorbell rings, who could it be?
Oh dear, it's Aunt Mary Lee!

Frosted wishes on the pine,
Kids all waiting for the sign.
Mittens lost, and then the fight,
Who stole cocoa from my sight?

Grandpa snoozes by the flame,
Dreaming of his deleted fame.
Each wrapped gift looks quite the mess,
Did the dog chew on this? Yes!

Firelight glimmers, shadows blend,
What is that? Oh no, my mend!
Odd socks packed for holiday,
'Twas a joke? Oh what a play!

A Glimmer of Hope and Cheer

Lightly wrapped in foil bright,
Elves are giggling with delight.
Pinecone hats and candy canes,
Who can guess these silly gains?

Reindeer games on rooftops high,
What a mess, oh my, oh my!
Wrapped surprises all aglow,
Guess my gift? A laugh or no?

Bells are jingling out of tune,
Silly hats now make us swoon.
In this laughter, doubts will cease,
Expecting joy, it brings us peace.

Ribbons flying, wrapped with love,
Wishing upon the stars above.
Each small gift brings funny cheer,
This chaotic time, the best of year!

Tinsel Tapestry of the Heart

Amidst the glitter and the cheer,
A cat's eye glimmers, who's this here?
Tangled lights weave quite a tale,
As dog chases shadows, wagging his tail.

Pine needles litter the festive floor,
Grandma sneezes as she wanders the store.
The cookies vanish, where could they go?
A little elf grins, putting on a show.

Funky sweaters and hats that clash,
A dance-off breaks out, oh what a bash!
With dad's moves, we cannot believe,
The whole room erupts, we're bound to achieve.

So here we gather, laughter to share,
These merry moments, beyond compare.
With joy we find, through the ride,
Life's quirks unite us, in our holiday stride.

Glistening Moments of Togetherness

Ribbons are tangled, why's it a fight?
The cookies are burnt, but hey, what a sight!
A cousin sings tunes, off-key and loud,
While auntie's asleep, she's dreaming proud.

Mismatched socks and a jolly old sleigh,
The gift wrap's a mess, it's quite on display.
The tree leans a little, it's quite the show,
With ornaments misplaced, as we laugh and glow.

Sibling squabbles over the last treat,
Each year it's the same, but we can't be beat!
We toast to the quirks and falls as we cheer,
Memories splashed with giggles and beer.

So hold your loved ones, let mischief flow,
Through tangled delight, we've come to know,
The spirit of laughter, so vibrant and bright,
These glistening moments make our hearts light.

The Fables Told Beneath the Boughs

In stories we gather, the wildest of dreams,
Like reindeers in tutus, or sleds without seams.
A hamster dressed up in a tiny red hat,
Dances a jig, it's a sight—imagine that!

With cocoa that's spilled and marshmallows gone,
We share the tall tales that muddle the dawn.
Grandpa's retelling, each time he forgets,
All giggles and snorts, it's a tale he'll regret!

The snowman outside is a real work of art,
With a carrot for nose, it's a culinary start.
But it's missing a scarf; it's looking quite cold,
While we warm our hearts over stories retold.

So gather around for the laughter to flow,
With fables so silly, in warmth we'll bestow.
Together we're silly, through every banter,
In this joyous season, we all are the lanterns.

Festive Reflections in Candlelight

Candles flicker, shadows dance,
Uncle Fred has lost his pants!
Grandma's cookies, slightly burnt,
In the frosting, a green ant squirt.

Laughter spreads like warm, bright cheer,
As the cat climbs up the reindeer.
A knocked-over tree, oh what a sight,
A family portrait gone awry tonight.

Wrapping paper, a giant mess,
Dog's found joy in our excess.
The laughter grows, a festive roar,
We just found Mom behind the door.

Candle's wax drips, a festive tide,
Lighthearted jokes we can't abide.
As long as love fills the space,
We'll remember this chaotic place.

A Tapestry of Holiday Wishes

Tinsel tangled in the hair,
Supervised by a cat with flair.
Mittens missing, socks askew,
Elves are dancing, who knew?

Cookies shaped like lopsided stars,
Dad insists he's driving cars.
Pine-scented candles light the air,
Why is Aunt Sue wearing a bear?

Mismatched lights blinking with glee,
Grandpa's snoring, can't you see?
The punch has poured, it's quite a sight,
Just one sip, and then the flight!

Wrapping gifts with too much glue,
Sounds just like a boisterous zoo.
Yet, within all this merry fun,
We celebrate, everyone!

Silent Snowflakes and Sparkling Lights

Snowflakes giggle, they spin around,
Grandpa's hat has lost its crown.
The lights outside blink in a row,
While a squirrel plots, oh what a show!

Jingle bells mix with silly tunes,
Achoo! We're blanketed by spoons.
The snowman winks with a melting grin,
His carrot nose found in the bin.

Minty treats fly through the air,
Mom's been sneaking, isn't that rare?
As children giggle in delight,
It's magic wrapped in this silly night.

Sparkling lights with colors bright,
Transform into a party sight.
As joy unfolds, in unexpected ways,
We'll cherish laughter in the days.

Wrapped in Magic and Mirth

Wrapped in laughter and cheer so bright,
A dancing elf steals a delight.
Presents overflow, a towering pile,
My little brother's cheeky smile.

With pet bows, the dogs prance near,
What's that noise? Oh brother, dear.
A gift unwrapped, a funny toy,
Creating endless fun and joy.

The kitchen's filled with holiday smells,
While Dad shares stories that no one tells.
"Where's the cake?" someone yells out loud,
Only to find it beneath a cloud!

In every hug and every jest,
We find our bliss, we find our rest.
Wrapped in magic, mirth, and love,
This holiday sparkles, bright as a dove.

Lanterns of Nostalgia and Cheer

A lamp flickers bright, oh what a sight,
Grandma's fruitcake, quite a delight.
Cats on the ledge, plotting their schemes,
A holiday chaos, bursting at seams.

Mismatched socks hang, humor in style,
Dance with the dog, just for a while.
Cookies are burned, smoke signals rise,
A laughter-filled kitchen, sweet holiday lies.

Lights twinkle like stars, but don't align,
Uncle Joe's jokes, aged like fine wine.
Gifts wrapped in paper, with dog's paw prints,
Searching for sanity, just in small hints.

So lift up your glass, let's toast the cheer,
For laughter and love, let's hold them dear.
Lanterns of laughter, memories flow,
In this wacky season, let's bask in the glow.

A Hearthside Christmas Reverie

A snowman's hat, slightly askew,
The dog decides to join in the view.
Santa on rooftops, rather clumsy tonight,
Tripped over a chimney, was quite the sight.

Hot cocoa spills, marshmallows afloat,
Cards from Aunt Edna, a cryptic note.
Family debates, who's cooking fish?
Grandpa claims he'll grant us a wish.

Mittens on hands, but socks on the floor,
We laugh as we find them behind the door.
Tinsel hangs low, and it surely reacts,
As the cat makes its leap, diving like an acrobat!

So gather around with glimmers aglow,
For stories and laughter, let's steal the show.
With warmth by the fire and joy on our faces,
This hearthside with you is where love embraces.

Whispers of Winter Lights

Winter winds blow, wrapped up real tight,
Our snowball fight turns into a sight.
Unique decorations made from odd bits,
A melting snowman, oh how it sits!

Cookies with sprinkles, a floury mess,
Mom finds the dog in her holiday dress.
Lights that won't blink, the whole street is dark,
We're left to admire our neighbor's remark.

Grandpa's tales, all mixed in with glee,
Of how he once wrestled a giant fir tree.
Siblings all giggle, slipping on ice,
One faceplant later, we'll think twice!

So here's to the laughter, the fun all around,
With whispers of joy, in moments we've found.
In winter's embrace, where mischief ignites,
We cherish the sweetness, the whispers of lights.

Tinsel Dreams and Candle Beams

Tinsel hangs low, giving a grin,
As the cat makes a jump, our patience wears thin.
Pine needles scatter, a messy delight,
Who knew the tree would become such a fright?

Candle flames dance, flickering cheer,
While Uncle Bob shares a tale loud and clear.
Eggnog spills down, oh what a scene,
The chaos and laughter reigns evergreen.

Gifts full of giggles, wrapped with love,
An ornament drops, the kind you don't shove.
Tickles and hugs beneath the lights' gleam,
In the midst of the laughter, we all dream.

So raise up your glasses, a toast to this time,
With tinsel and candle beams, all in rhyme.
In every mishap, let us always find,
Joyful adventures, a heart intertwined.

From Branches to Heartstrings

Pine needles dance and sing,
As ornaments spin with bling.
Cats plotting mischief with glee,
While grandma's lost her cup of tea.

Twinkling lights wrap around the room,
Little Timmy's built a broom.
There's tinsel tangled in my hair,
And Uncle Joe is in a chair.

The Glow of Togetherness

Cousins giggle, all aglow,
Playing pranks with mistletoe.
Soda spills on the floor again,
A game of tag with mom and Ken.

Grandpa's snoring in the light,
Where cookies vanish out of sight.
We share tales, both wild and tall,
And someone always dings the wall.

Joy in Every Gift

Presents wrapped with bows so tight,
Each unwrapped brings pure delight.
A pair of socks, oh what a find,
The look on Dad's face is one of blind.

A robot arm that won't behave,
And Auntie's fruitcake we must brave.
Giggles echo, laughter's free,
Each gift a chance for jubilee.

Tales of Frost and Warmth

Outside, the snowflakes start to play,
Inside, the roast is burning away.
With mittens stuck on puppy's paws,
He steals the scarf—we all pause.

Hot cocoa mugs with marshmallow fluff,
Mom claims her recipe is just enough.
But chaos reigns, as spills abound,
While holiday cheer is all around.

Whispers of a Frosted Night

In the attic, we found a strange shoe,
A relic of Christmas, but whose could it be?
It danced on the table like it owned the view,
While the cat took a leap, oh what a spree!

Mom hid the cookies, to save them from fate,
But caught in her hand, they vanished in mirth,
Did she just eat one? Was it then too late?
The crumbs told the story, of chaos and dearth.

The lights on the tree twinkle, catching the eye,
A squirrel at the window, just checking the scene,
With a wink and a nibble, he bids us goodbye,
Leaving us laughing, so merry and keen.

Wrap up the leftovers, don't let them get cold,
One bite of that fruitcake, and all will be clear,
With giggles and stories, the night we behold,
The cocoa spills over, but joy's ever near.

Secrets Wrapped in Satin

Presents peeking out with a ribboned embrace,
What's inside them? We all want to know,
Dad's secret is laughter, it's hard to erase,
His gift was a sweater, a real fashion faux!

Sister's surprises, they keep piling high,
But every unwrapping leads to her frown,
Last year's doll still gives her a sigh,
As she learns to embrace all her throwbacks down.

Uncles and aunts, they're all in their spree,
They bicker about who had the best roast,
Each claim gets louder; oh, can it be?
To see who will brag at the family post?

The room fills with giggles, the joy can't refrain,
The secrets, the laughter, they dance in the air,
As satin wraps hold memories, blissfully plain,
In this comic chaos, we joyfully share.

The Hearth's Embrace

The fire is crackling, its dance is a show,
With marshmallows roasting, in sweet, sticky melt,
Dad's face turns to ketchup, a curious glow,
He grabbed the wrong bottle, we're doubled in felt.

Huddled on couches, we spill tales so wild,
Forget the old stories, they've lost all their flair,
Now it's about Uncle, who once was just mild,
But in Christmas pajamas, his antics lay bare.

Let's sing some carols, a mix-up of tunes,
We dance in the glow, while the cat steals the socks,
With chants of good cheer, and silly balloons,
Our laughter erupts, spinning time like a clock.

As embers fade softly, we hug and we cheer,
The hearth's gentle warmth wraps us all tight,
In this laughter-filled moment, there's nothing to fear,
With memories made bright, and our hearts full of light.

Tinsel Dreams and Lullabies

Oh what's this, a tinsel-tangled mess,
Caught in the dog's tail, he prances with glee,
A glittering serpent, it causes some stress,
While we double-up laughing, oh can't you see?

The tree's dressed in jewels, yet something is wrong,
We check on the lights, where did they all go?
With teasing remarks, we break into song,
As Mom wonders why she's all covered in snow.

Cousins arrive with their wild-wrapped gifts,
Each one a puzzle, or wrapped with old maps,
Is this mine—or yours? Oh, watch as it lifts,
Our spirits so high, with belly-laugh snaps.

The night rolls on, with the clock chiming near,
We close with sweet dreams and some giggles still flow,
For all the mishaps, the joy shines so clear,
As love wraps around us, and laughter will grow.

Twinkling Tales of the Night

Lights are tangled in delight,
Cats are plotting a grand heist.
A dog jumps up with a fright,
Chasing shadows like a ghostly mist.

Gifts wrapped tight with bows so grand,
Unraveled by tiny hands at play.
Confetti from last year's band,
Turns the room into a circus sway.

Eggnog spills like holiday cheer,
Dad trips on the reindeer sleigh.
His face turns bright, no need to fear,
Laughter blooms where chaos lays.

While snowflakes dance on windows bright,
We share tales of long-lost socks.
Oh, what a scene, what a sight!
Funny faces grace the clocks.

The Warmth of Togetherness Aglow

Crackers pop with a festive whack,
Everyone reaches for the treat.
Uncle Joe, he'll not hold back,
With a joke that cannot be beat.

A gingerbread man starts to sway,
Dancing near the punch bowl's rim.
Grandma says, 'Just dance away!'
While Grandpa sways on a whim.

The fire crackles, casting light,
As we roast marshmallows on skewers.
A mouthful leads to a slight fight,
With sticky hands creating brewers.

Gather 'round, the carols rise,
A cat napping, a crinkled prize.
As faces glow in warm surprise,
We laugh until the joy complies.

Revelry in the Flickering Light

Little feet patter on the floor,
Chasing dreams with giggles galore.
A snowman hat, a pillow fort's door,
Imagination, the best encore.

Twinkle lights compete with glee,
As Dad struggles with a tangled mess.
Mom shakes her head, 'Oh, let it be!'
With a sigh of joyful stress.

Hot cocoa spills, the laughter flies,
With candy canes stuck in the couch.
'Tis the season,' the kitten cries,
As the dog hides from a playful slouch.

Each corner echoes a jolly tune,
As socks become hats on silly heads.
The magic sparked by a bright balloon,
Is why this night is truly spread.

Secrets Shared in Holiday Hues

Whispers float like the glitter flakes,
As secrets rustle the gift-wrapped walls.
A great debate of which cake bakes,
Reveals a pie that proudly calls.

With glitter trails on a puppy nose,
And wrapping paper covering the floor.
A faux pas in bows, I suppose,
Who knew gifts were made to explore?

The reindeer perch upon the shelf,
Pretending to judge all our fun.
"Oh dear," we laugh, "let's just be ourselves,"
And dance till the clock says we're done.

So here we sit, with full hearts bright,
As silliness reigns through the night.
With giggles sewn, oh what a sight,
These treasures are pure holiday light.

Festive Glow and Silent Snow

The lights are twinkling bright,
My cat thinks they're her toy.
She leaps and pounces with delight,
Oh, that furry ball of joy!

The cookies stacked too high,
I swore I'd leave them there.
But now I see them fly,
As I munch without a care!

The cardboard box is now my chair,
Each ribbon's a tangled mess.
I wear a hat as if to dare,
Who needs more than this fest?

Yet here we laugh and cheer the night,
As festive spirits sway.
The cookies—gone without a fight,
My waistline's in dismay!

Embrace of the Season's Warmth

With cocoa slightly spilled,
I sit and watch the show.
The dog has just been thrilled,
By snowflakes put on tow!

The scarf I knit last year,
Doubles as a maze.
I twist and turn in fear,
Just trying to impress!

Uncle Joe's big belly jig,
A shake with every laugh.
He tries to dance a jig,
And splits his festive scarf!

Amid the mittens lost,
And snowballs flying true,
We trade our winter costs,
For every laugh anew!

Glistening Moments in the Glow

The shimmer on the tree,
Like disco lights galore.
Last year's socks—who will see,
The list is getting more!

A present wrapped so tight,
It gifts me quite a grin.
I wonder if tonight,
I'll gift myself a win?

Mom's cooking on the stove,
A recipe gone wrong.
The smoke begins to rove,
And singing's not her strong!

Yet laughter fills the air,
With every little quirk.
The sparkle's hard to bear,
As all of us go berserk!

A Spectrum of Winter's Delight

The snowman wears my hat,
He looks a little sly.
With carrot nose and chat,
I swear he winked his eye!

The kids are throwing snow,
As I slip on the ice.
I might just steal the show,
With every tumble slice!

The cocoa's thick as glue,
I'm brewing one for me.
I think I'll add a few,
Marshmallows, just for glee!

Yet here beneath the stars,
We share our silly cheer.
With every little scar,
We laugh without a fear!

The Scent of Pine and Peppermint

The pine smells sweet, it's quite a treat,
A cat with tinsel caught on its feet.
Grandma's cookies, a sticky delight,
Oh, who knew frosting could start a fight!

Lights dance above with a frosty glow,
Dad's trying to rap, but he's moving too slow.
Ribbons unravel, oh what a sight,
I'll hide by the tree, just out of spite!

Advent's Delight in Twinkling Eyes

Calendars count down, oh what a race,
Every day brings a new goofy face.
Uncle Joe sings off-key, quite a tune,
While Cousin Max tries to eat the moon!

Stockings hang low, stuffed with sweet fluff,
Who knew that fruitcake could be so tough?
Sneaky snowmen in the yard stand still,
But watch out, folks, they're here for the thrill!

Radiant Moments Amidst Holiday Cheer

Laughter and joy twirl in the air,
A snowball flies, oh how unfair!
Silly sweaters with lights that blink,
Mom's favorite mug, okay, let's not think!

Snowflakes flutter, we race outside,
In search of the sled with the family pride.
Dad can't quite steer, we wobble and roll,
But we're doubly joyful, that's our goal!

Flickering Flames and Family Laughter

Candles flicker, shadows play,
Sister's dance moves steal the display.
Grandpa's jokes, they never grow old,
Though for the punchline, I'm yet to be sold!

Hot cocoa spills on the festive song,
While the dog steals a cookie, oh so wrong!
We gather round, joy on our face,
Deciding who's winning this silly race!

Joy in the Flicker of Candlelight

A candle's dance, so bright and bold,
My cat thinks it's a toy to hold.
With leaps and bounds, he plots his chance,
To pounce and twirl, a clumsy dance.

The wax drips down, a dripping foe,
My socks are safe, or so I know.
Then off he goes, with a great big leap,
He's found a spot, oh now I'll weep!

A strange parade of shiny things,
My dog thinks bells are birdie sings.
He howls along, a tuneful mess,
While I just think, "This is a jest!"

With every laugh, the night takes flight,
Candlelight's charm, a silly sight.
In every flicker, joy's our quest,
We'll giggle more, it's for the best!

Pine-Scented Reveries Unfold

The pine tree nods, its branches sway,
Reminds me of that fateful day.
With baubles strewn and tinsel bright,
I lost my shoe in the twinkling light.

My auntie's cat, with stealthy pride,
Thinks all the gifts are toys to hide.
She leaps on high, a furry spook,
Then runs amok, oh what a nook!

The smell of pine, a festive cheer,
Yet Grandpa's sneezes bring us fear.
He asks for tea, with humor sown,
As wrapping paper starts to moan.

In tangled lights, we find our fate,
The laughter echoes, can't be late.
With every twinkle, good times rise,
Who knew this chaos could be a prize?

The Symphony of Sights and Smiles

Oh what a sight, the floor's a maze,
Wrapped gifts scattered in a daze.
The dog's confused, he sniffs around,
While kids take turns to prance and bound.

My sibling shouts, "There's one for me!"
But finds a pair of socks, oh glee!
A sniff of pine, another cheer,
And then a cookie disappears!

The laughter rings, a festive tune,
As Grandma croons, her voice in boom.
A chorus formed by all our glee,
Like jumbled notes from a symphony.

With every stumble, giggle grows,
Who knew chaos could bring such prose?
In charming antics, our hearts align,
Note by note, our glee will shine!

A Cosmic Embrace of Joyful Nights

Stars are twinkling on this bright night,
A cosmic joke, oh what a sight!
Uncles spin tales that sprout and grow,
While juggling cookies, putting on a show.

The toast burns crisp, a smoky drama,
While laughter's scent is pure, like karma.
A dance of joy, as chaos thrums,
Who needs more when silly comes?

Relatives swap the funniest yarns,
As kids make faces, like little charms.
'Tis a night where socks become the fun,
In merry mayhem, we're never done!

Through all the giggles, we find our light,
Each smile a star, in velvet night.
And as we embrace, the jokes take flight,
What magic happens in joyful sight!

Secrets Cradled in Pine Fragrance

Beneath the branches, gifts piled high,
Cats plot their heist, oh me, oh my!
Tinsel glimmers, an enticing tease,
While dad's snoring sets the holiday breeze.

Elves in the pantry, sneaking some treats,
Maybe a cookie or two, oh what feats!
Santa's got a list, but not for the snacks,
Instead, he's checking if the kids are on tracks.

Bows on the packages, tied up with flair,
Last-minute shoppers in pajamas, beware!
Mom's gift-wrapping skills? A sight to behold,
Looks like a penguin wrapped in yarn and gold.

Lights twinkle wildly, up on the roof,
Neighbors eyeing our chaos, that's no spoof.
We giggle and snicker till late in the night,
In the glow of the season, we all feel the light.

Glowing Hearts and Twinkling Eyes

Mistletoe hanging, we give it a try,
Dad leaps with laughter, oh me, oh my!
We dance 'round the room, in socks and in cheer,
Grandma just smiles, with a twinkle, my dear.

Hot cocoa's a staple, spills on the floor,
The dog joins the party, then begs for some more.
With gooey marshmallows and laughter in spades,
A sprinkle of chaos, a dash of charades.

Wrapping up gifts, we mix up the tags,
Giving Uncle Fred a pair of new rags.
Sister's surprise? It's a glittery shoe,
One left for her brother, of course, just for you.

Laughter erupts from the living room bright,
All of our secrets exposed in the light.
With each quirky moment, our joys intertwine,
In this circus of fun, we've truly divine.

Tides of Light and Laughter

Candles all flicker, creating a glow,
The dog in a sweater, the cat steals the show.
Kids at the table, glitter all around,
With laughter erupting, pure joy can be found.

Presents all labeled, each one's a surprise,
But where did they hide all those holiday pies?
Mom's in the kitchen, her apron all stained,
With flour and sugar, her efforts unfeigned.

Snowflakes are falling, outside it's a dream,
Sledding all day, hot cocoa supreme.
Snowmen are built with a pineapple hat,
It's festive and silly, oh imagine that!

In the midst of the giggles, we all gather near,
Glass raised for a toast, with holiday cheer.
With stories of blunders and laughter alight,
This season of joy makes each heart feel so bright.

The Spirit of Giving Wrapped in Gold

Tangled up lights, what a glorious mess,
Batteries missing? Oh, what a stress!
Mom's searching frantically, with a sigh and a frown,
While dad's on the roof, breaking into a clown.

Cookies and milk left out for the night,
But cat's on the counter, eyeing them tight.
Stockings get stuffed with odd, little things,
Like socks and the strangest of trifling bling.

Family predictions, who'll snore out loud?
There's always one cousin, it's a family crowd.
With tinsel and laughter, all wrapped up with cheer,
We share stories of each silly moment right here.

So gather together, with warmth and delight,
In this wacky season, everything feels right.
With hugs and with giggles, we all know the rule,
The spirit of giving, it makes us the fool.

Memories Wrapped in Ribbon and String

Tinsel stuck in dad's sweater,
Momma's baking, always better.
Gifts that jingle when they fall,
Uncle Joe's snoring, loudest of all.

Cats meowing, sneaking a glance,
Presents piled high, what a dance.
A twist of fate in every bow,
Like Aunt Sue's hairdo, quite the show.

Grandma's fruitcake, a legendary tale,
One slice offered, courage must prevail.
Laughter echoes, fill the hall,
As cousins play, they trip and fall.

Memories thrive, oh what a fling,
Wrapped in laughter, oh the joy we bring.
With each giggle, a story to tell,
Tangled up in this festive spell.

Serenity Amidst the Festive Glow

Lights twinkle like fireflies' dance,
A salad of sprinkles, mistaken for plants.
Grandpa's jokes, just never land,
While the dog snags the gingerbread hand.

Pine scent mingles with cocoa delight,
Wrapping paper in every sight.
Mom's searching for scissors, oh what a plight,
While dogs trade the toys in a joyful fight.

Cousins giggling, wearing hats too bright,
Fairy tales woven into the night.
Finding peace in the chaos and screams,
Who's been naughty? Blame Auntie's dreams.

Serenity found in each twinkling light,
Where laughter and love take gloomy flight.
Wrapping this moment, so warm and bright,
As merry-go-rounds spin from day into night.

Luminous Hopes in a Winter's Embrace

Snowflakes swirl like a bouncing ball,
Mom's asking if you've eaten at all.
Creative gifts wrapped in chaos, a spark,
While the kitten jumps high, leaving a mark.

Mittens tangled and socks mismatched,
Whispers of secrets and gifts to be hatched.
Hope springs eternal in this winter's delight,
As we sing carols that sound just right.

Funny tales of Christmas past,
Like grandpa's beard, a fuzzy cast.
With every chuckle, warmth does embrace,
In this lively, loving, festive race.

Luminous hopes twirling with cheer,
Reflecting dreams of family near.
Wrapped in joy, each heart takes flight,
As laughter spills into the night.

A Tapestry of Light and Love

Jingle bells ringing a comical tune,
Bouncing off walls like a playful balloon.
Auntie's attempts at a holiday feast,
Kept more for laughs than a hungry beast.

Mismatched ornaments hang from the pine,
Granddad swears he once built a shrine.
Snowmen built with no sense of style,
Melting away, yet bringing a smile.

The dog snags a hat, a sight so grand,
Chasing the children, quick as he can.
Every moment a thread in the weave,
Creating charm one can hardly believe.

A tapestry spins, light shines above,
Woven with laughter and endless love.
Through this chaos, our hearts align,
In festival spirit, everything is fine.

Kindling Joy Amidst the Winter Chill

Snowflakes fall like tiny hats,
The dog wears one and chases rats.
Baking cookies, flour on my face,
As I slip and slide in my own place.

Jingle bells play a funky beat,
I dance around, can't feel my feet.
Mistletoe hangs, and I make a dash,
Kissing the cat is my only crash!

Neighbors laugh from across the street,
As I juggle gifts, a comical feat.
Tripping over ribbons, what a sight,
Laughter echoes deep into the night.

The lights twinkle, a sight to see,
While I wrestle with the Christmas tree.
With tinsel tangled, I proudly shout,
"Best decoration!"— then knock it out!

An Elegy to Joy Beneath the Lights

The stockings sag with snacks they hold,
And in my mind, I've struck gold.
Small hands reach in for sweets they find,
While parents hope their kids are kind.

A snowman stands, but he's a mess,
With carrot nose and a doughnut dress.
Kids start laughing, they're in a whirl,
And snowflakes fall— oh, what a pearl!

The tree lights blink like disco balls,
While dad tries to catch the cat that sprawls.
It's a comedy, our family play,
As we trip on wrapping while we sway.

Laughter bounces, there's nary a frown,
With cookies that make us tumble down.
In this parade of giggles and cheer,
We know that joy is always near.

The Taste of Wishes and Sugar Plums

Cookies burned; I just can't bake,
The fire alarm is wide awake.
Milk and chocolate spill with glee,
While the elves laugh out loud at me.

Let's hang the lights on roofs and trees,
I swear I saw my neighbors sneeze.
Frosty winks with a mischievous grin,
As I stumble back to the kitchen again.

Gingerbread men with jelly bean eyes,
Every mistake just adds to the highs.
A taste of wish, an oven's mishap,
But joy fills the air like a warm wrap.

Jingle all the way, I hear them say,
Though my plan went awry today.
With laughter shared, the spirit rings,
Even burnt cookies can have their flings!

A Cauldron of Cheer in Festive Nights

A pot of cheer, I try to brew,
Hot chocolate spills—oh, what a view!
Whipped cream clouds like snowflakes swirl,
As marshmallows dance and twirl.

The cat is tangled in the lights,
Wreaking havoc on festive nights.
I steady myself for a dramatic fall,
While reminders of jingle make us all haul.

We wear our sweaters, each a sight,
With reindeer playing in the night.
Socks that clash with a loud demand,
Squeezed with joy, hand in hand.

As laughter bubbles like cider's steam,
We find our joy, our gleeful theme.
In this cauldron, our hearts are bright,
With giggles and warmth through our shared delight.

Laughter Dancing in the Soft Glow

Tiny elves dance round the feet,
Spilling cocoa, oh what a treat!
Fido barks, he joins the play,
Swiping cookies, then runs away.

Giggles echo through the night,
Wrapped presents start to take flight!
A wish for socks, they mishear,
And gift a cat instead, oh dear!

Tinsel tangled in Uncle's hair,
As he juggles holiday flair!
Merriment fills the air we roam,
With joy and laughter, we feel at home.

Ribbons fly like straightened dreams,
While Auntie tries to catch the gleams.
Pinecone hats for every pet,
This Christmas fun we won't forget!

The Essence of Togetherness Illuminated

Grandpa's snoring by the fire,
A chorus of laughter rising higher!
Presents spill, all in a heap,
Poor Santa's lost, he's in too deep.

Mom's cooking brings a fragrant wave,
But the smoke, oh, it misbehaves!
Out pops the turkey, burnt and bold,
My brother's face, a sight to behold!

Matching jammies, what a surprise,
When Dad trips on Mom's holiday pies!
Sister's giggle turns into a roar,
As the dog slides right out the door!

Candles flicker with sparks of cheer,
While cousin Bob tries to steer clear.
Of dancing socks that sing out bright,
We sway together, a comical sight!

A Haven of Joy in Soft Embrace

Cookies baked but slightly burnt,
A masterpiece, or so we learned!
Santa's list is now a mess,
With socks and spoons—what the heck, I guess!

Children giggle, plotting their way,
To sneak a peak at gifts today.
But the cat takes a lead in play,
With glitter bombs to keep at bay!

Auntie's snort, we can't contain,
As she spills punch during the fun campaign.
Uncle's dance, a sight divine,
He's limping now, but he's still fine!

Wrapping paper tossed with glee,
As Mom declares, "Who let the dog free?"
We cheer and laugh, let chaos reign,
In joyful tunes, we'll sing through the pain!

Frosted Dreams Beneath the Glitter

Snowflakes twirl with laughter born,
Snowmen blink at every yawn!
Presents swap, then clatter loud,
With whispering secrets from every crowd.

A puppy barks, he wants to play,
While Grandma hides her spry ballet.
A toast with juice, we raise it high,
To Auntie's wig that just won't fly!

Gingerbread houses, what a sight!
Some towers lean, it's quite the plight.
Building forts through giggles shared,
In the bright glow, we've truly spared!

Ribbon fiasco, we stuff it right,
With laughter ringing through the night.
Family warmth, a joyful blend,
In every smile, our hearts extend!

Enchanted Evenings of Togetherness

On the floor, a cat takes a dive,
While unwrapped wonders come alive.
Tinsel tangled in the dog's tail,
As laughter erupts like a jolly hail.

Grandma's fruitcake makes its grand debut,
In shades of green and a rather odd hue.
Uncles dance, but they've lost the beat,
While kids giggle, sneaking a treat.

While socks descend like falling snow,
The neighbors peek in with eyes aglow.
A partridge chirps from the loudspeaker,
As dad tries to out-cook the sweet-talker.

We toast with mugs filled to the brim,
Watered-down cider, it's getting grim!
Yet in all the chaos, perfect bliss,
An enchanted night, we wouldn't miss.

Lights That Dance on Cold Nights

The lights twinkle like stars in a hurry,
While dad trips and calls it a flurry.
Mom's laughter spills from her hot cocoa,
As the kids play tag with the pizza dough.

The snowman outside leans a bit,
Waving a scarf that's slightly unfit.
A squirrel shows up for an audition,
Stealing a cookie; that's his mission!

Presents wrapped with bows that snag,
One misplaced gift, and we all gag.
Shrieks of joy, and then a sigh,
As we ponder who the gift's really for—oh my!

So on this night of chilly delight,
We laugh till it hurts, all feels just right.
With lights that dance, we share the tale,
Of our wild crew and the epic fail.

Cherished Moments Beneath the Boughs

An elf hat stuck on the family cat,
We laugh and snap photos of that.
With cookies missing—the mystery's in,
We all suspect the little twin!

A gift that rattles as someone struts,
Dad prays it's not more Christmas nuts.
We argue gently on who will sit,
To unwrap first, but oh, the wit!

Beneath the boughs, old stories told,
Of grandpa's goals and the pants that hold.
The ornament with a glittering fall,
Turns out it's just another dad's b-ball.

As things go flying, and laughter fills air,
Underneath it all, not a single care.
For cherished moments are found in glee,
With family gathered, just you and me.

Embracing the Spirit of Giving

The gift of socks—how did it fare?
A horror show lingered in the air.
A "thing" wrapped up with a riddle so neat,
Turns out it's Aunt Sue's three-legged seat!

We giggle and snicker at the sight,
As mom disturbs the dog's cozy night.
Each unwrapped treasure a new little tease,
It's the spirit of giving that aims to please.

Uncle Jim's plan to share a dance,
Fizzles out in a hilarious prance.
With mismatched socks, he twirls with glee,
As we all shout, "This is the best, you see!"

Through laughter and jests, the love will remain,
In moments like these, we all feel the gain.
For embracing this spirit brings joy that's divine,
With each quirky moment, our hearts intertwine.

Mirth and Magic in the Air

The cat climbed up with glee,
Knocked down gifts just to see.
Wrapping paper flies around,
As the dog runs, what a sound!

Uncle Fred trips on a toy,
Yells out loud, oh what a joy!
Cookies vanish, crumbs in tow,
Who ate them? Nobody knows!

Lights flicker, a funny sight,
Grandma's dancing, what a fright!
Snowflakes swirl while we all cheer,
For the best time of the year!

Laughter bubbles, hot cocoa spills,
Neighbors join with holiday thrills.
Mirth and magic fill the night,
In this festive, joyful light.

Enchantment Amongst the Spruce

Pine needles fall like confetti,
A squirrel's action? Quite unsteady!
We've left out snacks for good cheer,
But the raccoon showed up near!

Mom's sweater, Grandma's delight,
But it's got glitter—they might fight!
Dad's record spins, a funky tune,
While we twirl beneath the moon!

The ornaments play hide and seek,
With every giggle, laughter peaks.
Polar bears dance on the floor,
I think we need a bit more!

Magic swirls through every laugh,
In traditions, we find our path.
Enchantment among spruces tall,
With family, we have it all!

The Dance of Twinkling Stars

Twinkling lights on every side,
Grandpa's jokes, can't take the ride!
He's convinced he's still so spry,
But now he's wearing mom's tie!

Cousins battle in a snowball fight,
While uncles tell tales late at night.
Ice cream sundaes, what a treat,
Oh, watch out for that sticky seat!

Cookies shaped like goofy hats,
Silly stories of cousin cats.
Laughter rings with joyful glee,
Oh, what a sight is this spree!

As stars above begin to wink,
We gather closer, start to think:
The holiday's spark, ever so bright,
In our hearts, it feels just right!

Echoes of Laughter and Yuletide

Echoes rise from every room,
As we dance and banish gloom.
A toss of tinsel, what a sight,
Filled with giggles, pure delight!

The gifts stacked high, a great surprise,
Watch out! It's filled with quirky ties!
Mom's secret stash of fruitcake there,
Just our luck—who wants to share?

The cookies burned, a disaster bold,
But we tell tales that never get old.
With each laugh, our spirits soar,
In this chaos, we laugh some more!

So here's to fun from night till dawn,
With jokes aplenty, and grace withdrawn.
Echoes of laughter fill the room,
Joyous hearts dispel all gloom!

Time Stopped in a Winter Wonderland

Snowflakes dance, a comical sight,
Santa's sleigh takes an unexpected flight.
Reindeer tumble, giggling all around,
Elves are mimes in a snowy playground.

Frosty melts, no worries on his face,
While cocoa spills at a hurried pace.
Laughter bubbles in the chilly air,
Ho ho ho, I lost my winter wear!

Jingle bells play a slapstick tune,
A snowman trip turns into a cartoon.
Candy canes slip, they wobble and sway,
Who knew winter could be this cliche?

The snowball fight is a grand spectacle,
Winners dance, losers find it delectable.
With each giggle, time seems to stall,
In this land of chuckles, we'll never fall.

A Chorus of Stars and Wishes

Twinkling lights are a dizzying show,
Candles wobble when the breezes blow.
Wishes jingling in every song,
Who knew holiday cheer could feel so wrong?

Comets dash and collide in the sky,
Santa's GPS says, 'Oh me, oh my!'
Flying high with a questionable steer,
He shouts, 'This is why I stick to beer!'

Stockings bulging with socks and some toys,
Kids giggle, their laughter just noise.
But one little pup took the whole stash,
Now he runs, oh what a dash!

A chorus of stars starts to lose its shine,
When baking fails and cookies align.
With sprinkles everywhere, a sugary mess,
We'll laugh 'til next year, I must confess!

Memory Lane Dressed in Gold

Ornaments sparkle in reckless array,
Last year's leftovers come out to play.
Grandma's fruitcake takes center stage,
With a note: 'Not for young or old age!'

Photos unfold in a comic collection,
Each snapshot brings out a silly reflection.
Uncle Bob stuck in a tinsel tangle,
His holiday cheer looks like it's dangling!

A parade of stories, in sparkly bliss,
From epic fails that might make you hiss.
Dancing in reindeer jumpers so bold,
Laughing at memories, they make me feel old.

Wrapped with laughter, every tale retold,
Remember when we froze, but mom was a gold?
These moments come alive, a timeless jest,
In warmth and silliness, we find our best.

Seasonal Whimsy and Timeless Stories

Snowmen grinning with carrot-nose glee,
Holding hands with a pine tree, oh wee!
A sled ride that turns into a race,
With a snowbank kiss, what a silly face!

Mittens mismatched, swinging with flair,
A cat attempts to climb up in the air!
An ornament crashes with a comical clang,
While holly sprigs all do a merry twang.

Kids in pajamas, their faces aglow,
Fill the room with a joyful flow.
Singing carols, they misplace the tune,
While dad joins in like a drumming raccoon!

Telling tales of when we went out late,
Got lost in the fog, oh they won't abate.
With every chuckle of seasonal cheer,
We gather together, year after year!

Milton Keynes UK
Ingram Content Group UK Ltd.
UKHW021842151124
451262UK00014B/1274